CHRIST
IN THE
CRISIS

HE MAKES THE DIFFERENCE

By

Mary Ann Kiszla

Published by
In Him Publishing
18004 Sun Ridge Circle
Noblesville, Indiana 46060

In Him Publishing
18004 Sun Ridge Circle
Noblesville, Indiana 46060

Copyright © 2004 by In Him Publishing
All rights reserved.
This book, or parts thereof, may not be reproduced in any
form without permission.

ISBN: 0-9650415-9-x

First Printing

To my Father and His Son
You are the calm in the chaos,
a haven in the midst of havoc
and my refuge in the storm.

FOREWORD

We will have crises in ours lives. It's not a question of if, but when. Some are the 'pop up' variety. I get a lot of those. They abruptly spring up, but for the most part they can be taken care of rather quickly.

But others linger longer and have a far greater effect on our lives. They touch us deeply and things may never be the same again.

CHRIST IN THE CRISIS looks at how we respond to crises, struggle through them and what we can learn from them. That has a lot to do with how we get on with our lives after the crisis.

When we turn to Jesus Christ, the outcome will be far different than trying to go it alone. He takes us through the trying times to victory. We rise above them. Instead of being overcome by them, we are overcomers.

I pray that as you read this book, you are encouraged. When things look hopeless, he is your help and your hope.

TABLE OF CONTENTS

THE TAPESTRY OF LIFE

I was admiring a piece of tapestry recently. I noticed one side was a nondescript jumble of threads, but a beautiful pattern emerged on the other.

And I thought, that's what we're like. All the things that happen to us--good and bad -- are woven into the fabric of our lives.

The bleak and somber parts are represented by darker colors while the happier times shine forth in brighter hues. There seems to be a mixture of both. And just as the sorrow in our lives makes us appreciate the joyful times so much more, the contrast enhances the tapestry. Even the crises we face have their place. Here and there we see a burst of color that catches our attention.

We can't see how it all fits together yet. The Master isn't finished with us. We don't know the final result, but as Jesus works out his purpose for our lives, we see his fingerprints all over it as he tenderly, lovingly guides each thread into its place in the pattern. He is the one who holds our lives together.

And when the tapestry is completed, he holds it up for each of us to see. "This is your life. To me, it is a thing of beauty."

CHAPTER 1

IT'S HE, NOT ME

Apart from me you can do nothing.

John 15:5b

IT'S HE, NOT ME

One of the most penetrating, life changing lessons I have ever learned is *it's not what I do for God, but what he does in me and for me and through me.*

When I was praying one morning, the Lord brought the word *Godfident* to mind. I liked the sound of that and asked him what it meant.

"It's being aware of who I am and whose you are and what I do in you and for you and through you. Your confidence is to be in me, not you. It's not what you do, but what I do. Self effort does nothing. It doesn't last. What I do does. The only fruit that lasts is my doing it through you. It's not what you do for me, but what I do in you and for you and through you."

The psalmist wrote: For you have been my hope, O Sovereign Lord, my confidence since my youth.[1]

In Proverbs we read: for the Lord will be your confidence and will keep your foot from being snared.[2]

It's not what I do, but what he does. It took a while to fully grasp this teaching and for it to take

---

[1] Psalm 71:5
[2] Proverbs 3:26

root in me. His hard lessons always do. I've found head knowledge alone isn't enough. It has to penetrate my heart and that takes time. What a difference it made when this truth took hold of me. That's when I began to put it into practice and live it.

I wish I'd learned this earlier, but I'm thankful I know it now. What I can do is nothing compared to what he can. He is God and he is able. He simply asks me to be willing and available.

Think about the ramifications of his perspective. It goes against the grain. The world teaches us self-reliance. We can do anything we put our minds to. It's a matter of trying hard enough. But God tells us to rely on him instead. Trying harder and harder won't do it. Instead of thinking "I can do it" he says, "Let me do it."

Trust in the Lord with all your heart and lean not on your own understanding; in all your ways acknowledge him, and he will make your paths straight.[3]

We don't like to admit we need help. We want to be in control of our lives. If we happen to run into a few problems along the way, we can always turn to him then.

But that isn't how God intends it to be. He wants to be in control. He wants to lead and we are

---

[3] Proverbs 3:5-6

to follow. So often we run ahead on our own and ask him to bless what we're doing.

As I considered what he was teaching me, I began to see how infinitely better his way is than mine. There is no comparison. He is God who is all knowing. I am not. I don't know what lies ahead, but he does. He has the answer for any situation that comes along. I do not.

Under his tutelage, I don't have to wonder what to do. I submit to him and he shows me. He says, I will instruct you and teach you in the way you should go; I will counsel you and watch over you.[4] And he does. More and more, I realize how very much I need him.

The burden is off me and on him. Jesus said, " Take my yoke upon you and learn from me, for I am gentle and humble in heart, and you will find rest for your souls. For my yoke is easy and my burden is light."[5]

Imagine two horses yoked together pulling in different directions. They aren't going anywhere and become more and more agitated as each struggles to go his own way. When I am yoked with Jesus, I am to go in the same direction he is. He leads and I follow.

---

[4] Psalm 32:8
[5] Matthew 11:29-30

When the Lord is in charge, he fulfills his purpose for my life. He created me and he alone knows what that is. I do what he calls me to do. I no longer hold him back or resist him. *I've learned he will take me only as far as I choose to go with him.* He doesn't force himself on me. It is my choice. How much I miss and fall short when I insist on doing it my way. Self effort is a waste of my time and his.

Life- long habits are difficult to break. They become fixed and ingrained in us. It isn't easy to change. We didn't acquire them in a day, nor will we be rid of them instantly. Our attitude is, "I can do it," until we find ourselves in circumstances where we can't.

We visited our son, Bill, and his family down south recently and attended church with them on Sunday morning. During his sermon, the minister mentioned a young man from the congregation who had given his testimony the week before.

Dan told the group he had learned something about his relationship with Jesus Christ. There is a big difference between being committed to someone and being fully submitted to him; giving a part of yourself to him when he wants all of you. That's something to think about.

Jesus calls his followers to total surrender. Anything less is not enough. Halfway doesn't do it.

He said we can't serve two masters. How miserable we are when we try.

Have you ever noticed the Lord doesn't just tell us to do something? He also shows us how to do it. He lived the life he calls us to. What a tremendous example he is for us.

Jesus didn't have any problem submitting to his Father while he was here on earth.

He said, "For I did not speak of my own accord, but the Father who sent me commanded me what to say and how to say it…So whatever I say is just what the Father has told me to say."[6]

Jesus told his disciples, "Don't you believe that I am in the Father, and that the Father is in me? The words I say to you are not just my own. *Rather, it is the Father, living in me, who is doing his work.*"[7]

Likewise, Jesus told his disciples, "Remain in me, and I will remain in you. No branch can bear fruit by itself; it must remain in the vine. *Neither can you bear fruit unless you remain in me.*"[8]

---

[6] John 12:49,50b
[7] John 14:10 (Italics mine)
[8] John 15:4 (Italics mine)

"I am the vine; you are the branches. If a man remains in me and I in him, he will bear much fruit; *apart from me you can do nothing.*" [9]

Jesus didn't vacillate. He didn't say, "You can't do much without me." He said, "You can do nothing." There is a finality about that word. He says the same thing to us today as he did to his disciples. *It depends on him.* It won't work any other way.

We are do-ers by nature. We're accustomed to doing our own thing. Sometimes we struggle and labor so hard to produce fruit for the Lord, and all the while *he wants to do it through us*. He produces the fruit. We simply bear it. He does the work and he gets all the glory. There is no reason or room for pride on our part. None whatsoever.

Paul put it this way, "I have been crucified with Christ and I no longer live, but Christ lives in me. The life I live in the body, I live by faith in the Son of God, who loved me and gave himself for me." [10]

Consider for a moment what Paul was like before he met the Lord on the road to Damascus. He was the epitome of self effort. He was zealous to a fault as he chased down the followers of Jesus and had them put in jail. But when Paul met Jesus, his life was radically changed forever. The former

---

[9] John 15:5 (Italics mine)
[10] Galatians 2:20

persecutor became a dynamic proclaimer of the Gospel. The focus was off what Paul could do and on Jesus and what he wanted to accomplish through this young man.

When people were arguing about whether to follow Paul or Appollos, Paul said, "What's all the fuss about? We're just doing the jobs he assigned us to do. God is the one who gets the credit, not us." I planted the seed, Apollos watered it, but God made it grow.[11]

It's exciting to watch the Lord at work in the lives of his children.

Before we departed for our trip down south, we decided to return home by way of the east coast. We prayed about where and how long to stay and what to see and made all our reservations. As we headed inland, we stayed overnight in Greenville, South Carolina. We arrived early and were able to check into the motel and get our room right away. We then set out to explore the city that afternoon.

Early the next morning we went down for breakfast at the motel. The young woman who was setting up things apologized for being a little late in doing so. She seemed quite upset. I asked if there was anything I could do to help. She said no but that something bad had just happened to her that morning.

---

[11] I Corinthians 3:6

I asked if I could pray for her. When I did, she opened up and told me what had happened. She is a Christian and said whatever she does, she does it unto the Lord. She also has a street ministry and helps many others. The Lord prompted me to give her one of my books which just happened to be in the trunk of our car: YOU ARE PRECIOUS IN HIS SIGHT, Your Self Worth Depends On Him. As I handed her the book, tears came to her eyes and she thanked me for being obedient to the Lord. "I need this."

Then she remarked, "You're a Christian too. I noticed you and your husband when you checked in yesterday. I could tell you are the Lord's."

God knew this young woman needed to know how very much he loved her especially at that moment when she had been deeply hurt. Only God could have worked out all the details to bring us together at this point in time.

It also made me realize something else. We never know who is watching us. As Believers, we are witnesses to others whether we know it or not. I pray we are good ones. That incident makes me more aware of what I say and do. I want to be a reflection of Jesus.

There have been many times in my life when the Lord has nudged me to call someone. As I dialed the number, I wondered, "What am I going to say?" When the person answered, I told him who I was and that I had been thinking about him and had him on my heart. Often the other person asked, "How did you know I needed encouragement and prayer right now?" I didn't, but God did.

I've also found that sometimes he says 'do' and sometimes he says 'don't.'

As Christians, we are geared to reach out to others when they need help. A friend was coming home following surgery, so I hurried to the grocery to get supplies for making dinner for her and her family. As I set out the ingredients and proceeded to begin preparations, something didn't seem quite right. *I hadn't prayed about it.* It was just something you do when people need help.

I decided maybe I'd better stop and pray about it now. "Lord, don't you want me to take in dinner for my friend tonight?"

"No. I have someone else I want to do it."

"But, I always take in food when someone is sick."

"Not this time."

So I put things away. I felt kind of strange about not doing anything, but I've learned the Lord has his reasons. Later I found out the two hadn't been getting along and he used this to mend the breach between them. Had I insisted on doing my thing, I would have gotten in the way of his plans.

We can't even imagine what God wants to do in our lives or how he wants to use us to reach others for him. Even if we know, we can't do it. It takes him doing it through us.

I believe we go through several stages in our Christian walk.

When we first become Believers, we are aware of all the things God does for us. As new Christians, how encouraging that is. We are consumed with his love for us.

Then as our love for the Lord increases and we grow in him, we have a yearning to serve him, to do something for him. To reciprocate. And so we look for things to do. We want to show him our love, to give back to him.

But the closer we come to him and the more we learn about him and our lives are entwined with his, we realize he is the one who makes it all happen.

I know that apart from him I can do nothing. But I also know I can do all things through him who strengthens me.

He says, "You're right. You can't do it, but together we will.

<u>Points to Ponder</u>

Jesus said that apart from him you can do nothing.

What difference does that make in your life?

Have you ever had something happen that you knew only he could have brought it about?

Why is it hard for us to admit we need his help? What happens when we do?

<u>Prayer</u>

Father, I know that apart from you I can't do anything, but I can do everything through you who gives me strength. Sometimes I forget that and try to do it all myself. When I do, the load gets pretty heavy and I struggle under it. Help me to remember you want me to be Godfident and to let you be in charge. I come to you in the name of the one who is my example, Jesus.

CHAPTER
2

CRISIS – WHAT IS IT?

As Pharaoh approached, the Israelites looked up, and there were the Egyptians, marching after them. They were terrified and cried out to the Lord.

Exodus 14:10

CRISIS – WHAT IS IT?

When you hear the word, crisis, what's the first thing you think of? What is it? Unbelievable Pressure? Stress? Urgency? Something that has to be done right now? The Unexpected?

Webster defines crisis as: an emotionally significant event or radical change of status in a person's life.

An unstable or crucial time or state of affairs in which a decisive change is impending especially one with the distinct possibility of a highly undesirable outcome. A situation that has reached a critical phase.[12]

His definition covers a lot. Certainly divorce- the death of a marriage, or the death of one's spouse would fall into the first category. Your life changes dramatically. Instead of two sharing a life, now there is only one. If there are children, you become a single parent and are both father and mother. Not only are you grieving, but you try to help your young ones through the grieving process too. Much is expected of you and you wonder if you can cope with it. There's no time off since there is only one of you.

You may be thrust into responsibilities you aren't familiar with. Your mate used to take care of

---

[12] Webster's Ninth New Collegiate Dictionary © 1988

those. There is less income now and finances are strained. How will you get through this? Will it ever get better?

Even something as exciting as getting married can cause a few crises along the way. Just ask any bride or groom. The smallest details and decisions often become so critical that the joy of marriage is overshadowed by all that has to be done.

Whenever I see a bride or groom getting stressed out, I want to say, "Relax and let God be in charge. He does a much better job of it."

I had just graduated from college. Hank, my husband to be, was inducted into the Air Force a few weeks later and left for basic training out east. We planned to be married after that was finished and before he reported for his first tour of duty.

Since we didn't know the exact day when that would happen, we picked two separate dates, thinking one or the other would surely work out. The invitations were ordered and the printer awaited confirmation of the correct date.

The dressmaker had finished my wedding dress and it was stored at her house. Attendants had been selected and their dresses ordered. The flower girl and ring bearer were chosen. My roommate from college was to play a medley of violin pieces during the ceremony.

The reception hall was reserved as well as the church and organist, the cake ordered and all the various details were taken care of. *Or so we thought.*

On a Friday afternoon two weeks *before* the scheduled wedding date, I received a call from Hank informing me he had just gotten his orders and would be coming home that weekend on his way to Cheyenne, Wyoming where he was to report in by Wednesday. We would have to get married this weekend.

My first reaction was, "Not this weekend. There is no way we can pull everything together." I realized this was one of the most crucial decisions I would ever make in my life. Then I thought, "Yes we can. With the Lord's help we can do it."

My mother's comment was, "If we can get ready for a funeral in three days, we can get ready for a wedding." We didn't even have that long.

After we hung up and the shock wore off, I realized Hank probably didn't have his blood test, a prerequisite for getting married in Indiana.

I had no idea where to find him at the Air Force Base. He had called from the Officer's Club, but was leaving right away. I took a chance and called there and somehow got through to him. I explained that he needed a blood test before we could get our marriage license. I had just gotten my test results back from the state. It takes three days to do so and we didn't have three days. However, I remembered there is little town in the northern part of the Indiana that gets around the situation. You can have a blood test taken and get the results back the same day. That would work for us.

The rest of that Friday was a whirlwind Everything had to be changed. We would be getting married on Sunday. The minister and church were available. We waited until after the church service was over, practiced in the afternoon and got married that night. Fortunately, the reception hall was also available on the new date, and the cake baker as well.

We had a little problem getting my wedding dress, however. The woman who had made it was out of town and wouldn't be back for two weeks. My dress was locked up in her house. I remembered she had a cat and thought about who might be taking care of it. I called a friend of hers and he let us in to rescue the dress. There wasn't time for invitations to go out so we put a notice in the local paper announcing our change of plans and the new wedding date.

Hank left the base shortly after I called, drove all night and arrived at my house very early Saturday morning. After sleeping a few hours we headed north to get his blood test and our marriage license.

The bridesmaid's dresses hadn't arrived yet, so we stopped by the out of town dress store Saturday to pick them up on our way back to my house.

Then Hank headed to his hometown up north to inform his parents of the switch in plans. He'd been so busy he hadn't told them yet. You can imagine their shock and surprise. Their son was getting married the next day. They took it quite well, however. I can imagine how they must have felt. Hank also had to scurry around to inform his best man of the new date and also to get another attendant.

My friends had planned a shower for me that Saturday night so I went, came home and packed the rest of the night for our trip out west.

What was the outcome? How did things turn out? The wedding proceeded without a hitch. Hank and I drove to the church together and were completely relaxed. With all that was going on, there was no time to worry. The important thing was getting married. It was all in the Lord's hands and he took care of it perfectly. As I look back and see how he worked everything out in such a short time, I am amazed. But then, he is God. Nothing is too hard for him.

What brings about a crisis? Various things. As I write this, our state has been deluged with rain for the past several days that resulted in much flooding. In our town, we broke the record for the amount of rainfall in one day. Even the forecasters admitted they didn't see this one coming. The devastation was totally unexpected and widespread. Roads were washed out, homes flooded and caked with mud and muck, even those that weren't in a flood plain.

Some cars attempting to maneuver through water covered streets were swept off the road into the raging streams. There was the loss of one life when they couldn't reach the victim in time. Another was rescued after sixteen hours in the water as he held on for dear life. The cleanup will take weeks, months or even longer. The physical and financial cost is great, but the mental and emotional strain is even greater. Lives will never be the same. That's one Labor Day weekend we will never forget.

What else causes a crisis? The loss of a job can result in dire financial straits. How do you pay the bills when there is no income? With company buy outs and down sizing you could find yourself unemployed along with many others. At fifty, you may be considered too old for that position – they can always hire someone younger to take your place for less money—and you're too young to retire. To add to the dilemma, you recently purchased a new home and it isn't paid off yet. What do you do?

Serious illness creates a great deal of stress whether it's yours or a loved one's. The day to day uncertainty takes its toll on all of you. It seems the only time you get out of the house is to go from one doctor to another. You don't even want to think about what the future holds.

When a crisis hits, it's often unexpected and sneaks up on us. Many things happen that we have no control over, but others we may bring upon ourselves.

When I was in college, I was assigned a term paper to be completed by a certain date. My grade for that class depended on it. Unfortunately, the paper was due after the Spring Break. I would have been much better off preparing it before the vacation. I had gathered most of the material before going home, but still couldn't find all that I needed. This was back in the "olden days" before the advent of computers. I put off working on the project during the respite thinking I could get it done very quickly when I returned to school. That was mistake number one.

Mistake number two happened after my return to campus. The fellow I was pinned to, now my husband, called from his school and decided to come up to see me on the day I had planned to dig in and finish the project. How could I turn him down?

I thought Hank would never leave. After he departed, I barricaded myself in my room and started in. I soon realized I had completely underestimated the magnitude of this undertaking. There was absolutely no way I could finish it in time. There weren't enough hours left to do so. Not only was there a great deal of typing required --of the old fashioned ilk-- but also drawings were to be included. I would have to pull an all-nighter.

You need to realize I don't do well late at night. For finals I would study until I got tired, then get up at four in the morning to cram some more. I'm more alert in the a.m. During four years of college, that worked quite well for me. But not this time.

The later the hour, the slower I typed and the more mistakes I made. Running out of whiteout was a big concern. I could scarcely keep my eyes open, let alone concentrate on what I was doing.

Somehow I completed the paper just as the light of a new day was dawning. After showering to wake me up and grabbing a bite of breakfast, I ran off to class to turn it in on time. I vowed then and there never to let that happen again. I had no excuse. I brought that crisis on myself.

Through the years, I have finally learned not to take on more than I can handle at one time. When asked to so something, I pray about it first. If the answer is 'no', I've found there is always a good reason for it. I don't know what lies ahead, but God does. Overburdening ourselves often leads to stress and crises when we are unable to accomplish what we set out to do.

Lately the Lord has been telling me: *"Don't major in the minors. Major in the majors."* He doesn't expect me to do everything, but to look at those things I need to do – the high priorities for each day. Just as I delete the spam and junk mail that invades my computer, I weed out those things that take up my time and yield little in return.

Things will happen to you. Crises will come along, but how you respond or react to them makes all the difference. What are you going to do when there's a crisis in your life? Are you going to put it in the Lord's hands or keep it in yours?

Have you ever thought about Moses as he stood there beside the Red Sea with the people of Israel? Pharaoh and his army were right behind him breathing down his neck.

As Pharaoh approached, the Israelites looked up, and there were the Egyptians, marching after them. They were terrified and cried out to the Lord.[13]

The Israelites complained bitterly to Moses. "Didn't we say to you in Egypt, 'Leave us alone; let us serve the Egyptians'? It would have been better

---

[13] Exodus 14:10

for us to serve the Egyptians than to die in the desert!” [14] They gave him no support at all.

Moses and the Israelites were trapped by the sea and their enemies. There was no place to go, no one to turn to except the One who really mattered. What did Moses do? Did he panic? *No, he gave the people hope.*

Moses answered the people, “Do not be afraid. Stand firm and you will see the deliverance the Lord will bring you today. The Egyptians you see today you will never see again. The Lord will fight for you; you need only to be still.” [15]

He had faith in his God. He trusted him before God did a thing. That says a great deal about his relationship with his Lord.

Moses told the people to watch and they would see God’s almighty power at work. He wasn’t just hoping God would come through. He knew he would. That’s faith. Being sure of what we hope for, certain of what we do not see. His faith was in a faithful God.

Then the Lord said to Moses, “Why are you crying out to me? Tell the Israelites to move on. Raise your staff and stretch out your hand over the

---

[14] Exodus 14:12
[15] Exodus 14:13-14
[16] Exodus 14:15-16

sea to divide the water so that the Israelites can go through the sea on dry ground.[16]

Moses did what God told him to do and God parted the waters and his people walked to the other side on dry ground.

Then the Lord said to Moses, "Stretch out your hand over the sea so that the waters may flow back over the Egyptians and their chariots and horsemen." Moses stretched out his hand over the sea, and at daybreak the sea went back to its place. The Egyptians were fleeing toward it, and the Lord swept them into the sea. The water flowed back and covered the chariots and horsemen – the entire army of Pharaoh that had followed the Israelites into the sea. Not one of them survived.[17]

That was quite a crisis, but *God took care of his people. He still takes care of us today as we turn to him.*

God answers when we call to him. He says, "I am bigger than any crisis. I will see you through whatever comes."

____

[17] Exodus 14:26-28

<u>Points to Ponder</u>

What causes crises in your life?

Are they the 'pop up' kind that spring up abruptly and are over quickly or those that linger longer and seem as though they will never end?

How do you handle them? What can you do about them?

<u>Prayer</u>

Father, this has been one of those days. From the moment I got up this morning, it's been one thing after the other. It doesn't seem to end. I try to do all I can, but that isn't enough. I need your help. Please show me what to do. I know you have the answer to this. You always do. I come to you in the name of Jesus, who always intercedes for me.

CHAPTER
3

WHO DO YOU TURN TO?

But I trust in you, O Lord; I say, "You are my God." My times are in your hands;

Psalm 31:14-15a

WHO DO YOU TURN TO?

Who do you turn to when you find yourself in a crisis? How do you get through it?

I was several months pregnant with our third child. The little girl across the street got the mumps and it was quite likely our two sons were exposed to them too. My doctor suggested giving me a shot to prevent me from getting them which he did.

One morning a few weeks later I woke up with a very painful earache. I called the doctor's office to see what medication I could take to relieve it. His nurse answered and listened to my problem and insisted that I see the doctor before taking anything.

I explained my husband was out of town on a business trip and I had no means to get there, but she kept insisting that I come in. She wouldn't take no for an answer. It's a good thing she didn't. Finally I asked a neighbor if she would drive the boys and me to the doctor's office. Very reluctantly she agreed to do so.

When the doctor examined me, the first thing he said was, "You have the mumps."

I replied, "But I can't have the mumps. You gave me a shot that was supposed to keep me from getting them."

" Shot or no shot, you have the mumps. When you get home, stay off your feet until you are completely over them. It is very important that you do so."

I didn't know whether to laugh or cry. How do you stay off your feet when you have a three year old and one less than a year who depend on you? Who was going to take care of them?

When I got home, I called one of our baby sitters and explained the situation to her. She was kind enough to come over right away but could only stay a few hours as she had another baby sitting job that evening.

When Hank called later that night I related all that had happened. He cut his trip short and returned home the next day.

After what seemed an eternity, I was finally over the mumps, but I had a lingering concern for our baby. Would he be all right? Had the mumps harmed him in any way?

Whenever I questioned the doctor about it, he said we wouldn't know until the baby was born. This was before hospitals had the state-of-the-art equipment and facilities they do now. The uncertainty was difficult to deal with. *I went through the rest of the nine months not knowing how things would turn out.*

What can you do at a time like that? Who do you turn to? I turned to the Lord. He was the One who encouraged and sustained me through all those long months of uncertainty.

But I discovered we weren't through with crises yet. Six weeks before Tom was born, I was hospitalized with kidney spasms. They put me in the labor room since they were afraid he might be born prematurely. Fortunately, he was not. As I left the hospital to go home, the nurse said, "I'm so sorry it was a false alarm and you didn't have your baby." I wasn't. We needed those extra weeks.

Tom was born early on a snowy February morning, just after midnight. I was so relieved and grateful to have delivered a healthy baby boy. The day we came home from the hospital there was a big blizzard and everything was blanketed in white. We had a hard time getting up our driveway and barely made it into garage. Our electricity didn't go off, but neighbors across the street were without power for several days. The Lord was looking after us.

With all that had happened, we assumed the worst was over, but it wasn't. A week later, I noticed a large ominous looking red blotch on Tom's chest that kept growing bigger and bigger. When we took him to the doctor, he said, "Get him to the hospital right away. He has staph infection."

We didn't realize there was a staph epidemic in many hospitals at that time.

At two weeks of age, Tom underwent surgery to remove the huge ugly growth on his chest and he was given a fifty/fifty chance of recovering. Had the infection spread inside his body through the blood stream rather than on the outside, he wouldn't have had a chance.

How fragile life is. It was a very wrenching experience to watch our son as he lay in the isolation ward fighting for his life. When he was a little older, I told him the long incision he has on his chest is his battle scar, a sign of victory. He made it!

During the first year of Tom's life we had many anxious moments nursing him back to health and taking preventative measures to keep his two brothers from also becoming ill.

Many babies born at the same hospital during that time contacted staph and some died. We later learned the infection was due to carelessness. It was traced to one nurse who did not wash her hands as she went from patient to patient and quickly spread the disease.

As I look at our son today, I am extremely grateful for still having him here with us. I think of how far the Lord has brought him. Last year, we had the privilege and joy of seeing Tom and Nichole married.

I learned some valuable things during the ordeal of Tom's illness that I still carry with me today. It was in times like these that I got to know the Lord better. I depended on him day by day.

The Scriptures began to mean even more to me as I related them to my life. They were written many years before, but they are still very relevant today.

I sought the Lord, and he answered me; he delivered me from all my fears.[18]

The Lord is close to the broken-hearted and saves those who are crushed in spirit.[19]

Prayer became a daily staple in my life as I turned to him more and more for his strength and encouragement and guidance. It still is.

I learned more about the Lord's love for me and for each of us. I knew he was and would always be there for me. When you've been through a crisis with someone, you grow closer to him. When he says "Draw near to me and I will draw near to you," he means it. I believe him when he tells me to cast my cares on him because he cares about me.

My love for the Lord grew as I got to know him better. I found out he is an ever present help in trouble. I can count on him. But he is more than

---

[18] Psalm 34:4
[19] Psalm 34:18

that. He is life itself. The quality of my life depends on where he is in it.

It is exciting to see him at work. That's something I never take for granted. It's an awesome thing to see the Lord God Almighty reach down and touch lives here on earth.

From heaven the Lord looks down and sees all mankind; from his dwelling place he watches all who live on earth – he who forms the hearts of all, who considers everything they do.[20]

I've also found that an on-going crisis wears you down. When you're going through a crisis, your whole system is on alert, all tensed up for action. The stress level is exceptionally high. If it is prolonged, your health often deteriorates over time. Crisis takes its toll.

What we need is a place of peace and security right in the middle of it. The Lord is that calm in the center of the storm. He is the One who holds everything together, including our lives.

I often think of those who work in the emergency rooms or trauma centers. Every patient who is brought in to them is in dire need of help. It's a place of constant crisis. When they leave the hospital and go home, how are they able to turn off the adrenalin and get back to 'normal'. Then how do they rev up again for work the next day?

---

[20] Psalm 33: 13-15

We have friends who find this time of life is very bleak. Some have been going through a series of illnesses for a long, long time. It's one thing after the other. Will it never end? They're almost afraid to think about tomorrow and what it may bring. Instead they concentrate on the day at hand and just getting through it.

Today I heard from a friend who recently found out he has an abdominal aortic aneurysm. They told him it's so large that it may blow at any time. He says he feels like a walking time bomb ready to explode at any moment.

Right now he is waiting to hear from the doctor to see if he is a candidate for stents rather than the more drastic traditional procedure. Immediate surgery is indicated. It's not a matter of if he should have surgery, but rather what kind.

He and his wife even have an emergency plan if something happens at home. The doctor told them they have less than twenty minutes to get to the nearest hospital. In the meantime, he waits with a great deal of fear and trepidation wondering what the future holds for him.

That isn't the only medical crisis this family has had in recent years. He and his wife, have both had cancer. At the present time test results show they are free from it. And each has had serious ailments before this.

As I pray for them, I wonder, "Lord, how much more can they take? How can they keep going? They have been through so much. Please give them some relief. Please heal them and give them hope."

Where do they find their help and hope? Doctors can only go so far. They may help the physical body and alleviate the pain, but something more is needed. His name is Jesus Christ. He is their help. He is their hope. He is the One who holds their life together. And best of all, they can take him along with them wherever they go.

These are the times when we also discover the dark clouds do have a silver lining. Good can come out of the worst of times. When we are at our weakest and have nowhere else to turn, he is there waiting to comfort and console us and see us through the troubling days ahead.

Paul said, "When I am weak, then I am strong." In his weakness he depended on God's strength. He no longer depended on his own.

These are the times when the Lord takes us in his arms and says, "It's all right. I am with you." That's what he said to me as I faced surgery many years ago. And when he did, his love and peace filled my very being. These are the times he draws us close to him and he reveals himself to us as he never has before.

He says, "I will never leave you or forsake you." And he won't.

And we reply, But I trust in you O Lord; I say, "You are my God. My times are in your hands;" What better hands could we be in than his![21]

---

[21] Psalm 31:14-15a

<u>Points to Ponder</u>

Who do you turn to when you're facing a crisis?

How do you get through it? And where do you find a place of calm in the middle of it?

What can you learn from the crisis? What good can come out of it?

How does it change your life?

<u>Prayer</u>

Father, there is no one else to turn to but you. You are my only hope in a hopeless situation. You are my refuge in the middle of the raging storm. You are the one I cling to. You are the one who will bring me through this. I trust you with my life. I come to you in the name of your Son, Jesus, who holds my life together.

CHAPTER
4

COUNT IT ALL JOY!

Consider it pure joy, my brothers, whenever you face trials of many kinds, because you know that the testing of your faith develops perseverance.

James 1:2-3

COUNT IT ALL JOY!

Do you ever read Scripture and think, "There is no way I can ever live like that." For me, a passage in James falls into this category.

Consider it pure joy, my brothers, whenever you face trails of many kinds, because you know that the testing of your faith develops perseverance. Perseverance must finish its work so that you may be mature and complete, not lacking anything.[22]

I'm still working on this one. I don't know about you, but I find it difficult to consider it pure joy when trials come along. I'd much rather do without them and omit them altogether. To make matters worse, the writer doesn't say 'if' he says 'when' knowing that whether we like it or not we are going to have them.

God's perspective on trials is different than mine. He looks at them as a way to test my faith and teach me what I need to know, to grow me in him and to equip me for whatever comes along. While my first thought is, "I don't need this. With all that's going on, Lord, I do not need this disruption right now."

Testing very quickly turns the spotlight on my faith. How strong is it? Will it hold up in the tough times? Do I trust Him in this? Can I endure

---

[22] James 1:2-4

to the end? Will I pass the test? Sometimes I don't do too well and I have to repeat the same lesson again until I get it right. For me, perseverance is one of those lessons.

Take computers for example. They are very helpful when they work correctly and a real pain when they don't. I use my computer for our business – for writing books, seminars, talks, correspondence with our distributors, just about everything. I especially depend upon Microsoft Word.

Last Saturday I was working on this book about crises. I decided to take a short break and get away from it for a little while. The system was working perfectly when I left, but when I returned I was unable to pull up Word. In fact, it froze every time I tried. I kept getting the message, "The system is dangerously low in resources." What did that mean? The only way I could exit was via the power source.

I made numerous attempts to get back into Word, but nothing worked. Since it was the weekend, I waited until Monday morning to call for help. Forget the on line support. I needed a human being and soon. Unfortunately the lines were clogged with inquiries about the Blaster worm virus. Finally I got through and talked with a real person only to be referred from one number to another. I used my cell phone as most of these were not 800 numbers.

On the fifth referral I thought I had found the party I needed to talk with but he was in customer service and could not really help with the problem confronting me. However, he gave me a service number, charged me $35 up front on my credit card and was about to refer me to a 'tech' who would show me what to do. Before he did that, however, my cell phone began to beep indicating it was about to fade out. I relayed this problem to the service rep and he gave me a number to call when I got it recharged. *I was so close to getting the problem solved and yet so far.*

Later, back with a fully charged phone, I dialed the new number he had given me. A recording came on suggesting online support, a step by step message on how to build a firewall and to get rid of the Blaster virus. Then instead of telling me to stay on the line for the first available person, it said, "If you get a busy signal, hang up and try again." After countless futile attempts, I finally reached a tech a little before 7 p.m. After a slow laborious process, Word was finally restored.

Had I not needed it so desperately, I might have been tempted to give up. I did not however, but persevered until the very end. The process I went through can best be described as one of total frustration until the problem was fixed. Then I felt relieved, grateful and filled with the joy of success.

However, I don't think that was what James had in mind. I was glad when the crisis was over and Word was back to normal. He meant I am to count it all joy even when I am going through it. I am to be joyful in spite of the problem, not because of it.

Counting it all joy when I am faced with a crisis over which I have no control, says a lot about my relationship with the Lord. Only as I turn the situation over to Him, is joy possible. It's his joy in me.

Joy is an attitude of the heart. We can't work it up ourselves. As we choose to be joyful, he fills us with his joy. That's how Paul could rejoice when he was in prison. No matter where he was, the Lord was there with him. He is there for us too. No matter what.

I've found there is a big difference between happiness and joy. Sometimes we get them mixed up. Happiness depends on what's going on around us or happening to us. If it's good, we're happy. If it isn't, we're not.

On the other hand, joy doesn't depend on our surroundings or circumstances. It has everything to do with Him. He is the One who gives us joy.

Joy is there in the middle of the problems. We can be joyful because the Lord is there with us. There is joy in his presence. Jesus went through trying times. He knows what it's like. He is able to help us through the trials and afflictions we face.

Why is joy so important? It's good for our health. A cheerful heart is good medicine, but a crushed spirit dries up the bones.[23]

Joy pleases the Lord. When we're joyful in the trials, it means we trust him to take us through them.

It is also a witness to others. They watch us closely. Does our faith hold up? When it does, it is an encouragement to them.

When facing affliction, rather than questioning why this is happening, I ask, "What are you teaching me through this, Lord? What do you want me to learn?" The first focuses on me and the problem, the second on Him.

What difference does it make how I react to adversity? This life is a testing ground. Will I choose God's way or another? His way leads to life. Every decision I make either draws me closer to him or takes me farther away.

You have made known to me the paths of life; you will fill me with joy in your presence.[24]

____

[23] Proverbs 17:22
[24] Acts 2:28

I want to see God's power in my life. I've learned challenges are usually part of the package. Without the challenges, I may think I don't need him then. I can get along on my own. There is always the danger of self effort. In the trials and tribulations, I know I need him. I am well aware that I am weak but he is strong.

The psalmist wrote: When I said, "My foot is slipping," your love, O Lord, supported me. When anxiety was great within me, your consolation brought joy to my soul.[25]

He also said: The Lord is my strength and my shield; my heart trusts in him, and I am helped. My heart leaps for joy and I will give thanks to him in song.[26] When was the last time you were filled up with joy?

It is comforting to know there is Someone who sees and understands. I will be glad and rejoice in your love, for you saw my affliction and knew the anguish of my soul.[27].

What happens when we go through trials? What do they do for us? Better yet, what do they do *in* us?

Not only so, but we also rejoice in our sufferings, because we know that suffering

---

[25] Psalm 94:18-19
[26] Psalm 28:7
[27] Psalm 31:7

produces perseverance; perseverance, character; and character, hope. And hope does not disappoint us, because God has poured out his love into our hearts by the Holy Spirit, whom he has given us.[28]

There's that word perseverance again. It's important to God that we persist in doing what he tells us to. He doesn't want us to give up. *Character counts with him.* He looks on the inside, at our heart. He wants us to become more and more like his Son, Jesus. As we endure, we have hope and that hope is in him alone. When Jesus was referring to the seven churches in Revelation, he kept stressing: He who stands firm to the end.

Philippians is often referred to as the book of joy. Throughout its pages, Paul talks about rejoicing. That's amazing considering the fact that he wrote it from prison. Joy is the last thing most people in his circumstance would think of. How could he do that? Because his eyes were firmly fixed on Jesus.

The Lord calls us to: Be joyful in hope, patient in affliction, faithful in prayer.[29] And to: Be joyful always; pray continually; give thanks in all circumstances, for this is God's will for you in Christ Jesus.[30] Are these impossible aspirations?

---

[28] Romans 5:3-5
[29] Romans 12:12
[30] I Thessalonians 5:16-18

They are words to live by, but can we? Not apart from him. Not without his help.

I have seen two people facing similar crises but with far different results. One became bitter and caustic and continually lamented her bad fortune. She never got over it.

"God, why did you let this happen? How could you do this to me?"

But the other one, who was also greatly grieved, turned to her Lord and Savior to see her through the heartache and pain.

"Lord, I need you. I can't make it through this without you. I have no one else to turn to, nor do I want to. Thank you for always being there for me, especially now. I don't know how things are going to turn out, but I trust you for them."

Grateful for his presence and strength through troubled times, she now reaches out to others as they go through their own fiery trials.

One does not move beyond what happened in the past. The other looks forward to what God has for her in the future. She knows whatever it is, it will be good because he will be there.

Hope in the Lord does not disappoint us. People let us down and so do things. He does not. Without hope, the soul withers. It looks to the past, not to the future. There is no joy, no expectation of what can be. When our hope is in him, we are refreshed and renewed and filled with his joy .

…but those who hope in the Lord will renew their strength. They will soar on wings like eagles; they will run and not grow weary, they will walk and not be faint.[31]

If you are going through trying times right now, I pray: May the God of hope fill you with joy and peace as you trust in him, so that you may overflow with hope by the power of the Holy Spirit.[32]

There are no better hands to be in than his.

One of the passages of Scripture I read and think about often is in Habakkuk. Though the fig tree does not bud and there are no grapes on the vines, thought the olive crop fails and the fields produce no food, though there are no sheep in the pen and no cattle in the stalls, yet I will rejoice in the Lord, I will be joyful in God my Savior.[33]

In spite of all that's happening, when nothing seems to be going right, I will still praise him. Together we will come through this.

---

[31] Isaiah 40:31

[32] Romans 15:13

[33] Habakkuk 3:17-18

<u>Points to Ponder</u>

How is it possible to count it all joy when you're going through trials? That's the last thing you feel like doing.

What happens when you do?

What difference does it make how you react to adversity?

How does that affect your life?

<u>Prayer</u>

Father, it's hard to be joyful at a time like this when everything is going wrong. I know it helps when I am, but I can't work it up myself. Would you fill me up with your joy? There is joy in your presence, when you are with me even in the middle of the storm. I come in the name of Jesus, the One who stilled the storm.

CHAPTER
5

HIS WAYS ARE DIFFERENT

"For my thoughts are not your thoughts, neither
are your ways my ways," declares the Lord.

Isaiah 55:8

God tells us quite plainly that his ways are different than ours.

"For my thoughts are not your thoughts, neither are your ways my ways," declares the Lord. "As the heavens are higher than the earth, so are my ways higher than your ways and my thoughts than your thoughts."[34]

We may not understand them. We may disagree with them, but he says they are far better than ours. After all, he is God and he is all-knowing. He is also love.

I wonder what it will be like when we meet him face to face one day. Will we finally comprehend those things that have puzzled us through the years? Will the enigma be solved? Will we say, "Now I see. Why didn't I think of that?"

I've come to the point where I simply trust in the character of God and all that he is. I believe he wants his best for me and only he knows what that is.

I used to sit down early in the morning and write out all the things I wanted to accomplish that day. However, I have learned there is a much better way. Now I ask the Lord what his priorities are for

---

[34] Isaiah 55:8-9

me. It's interesting to note that many of the things I thought were so important are not to him. Those I hadn't even considered often top his list for me to do. There is one that never changes, however, and that is my time with him. That comes first before everything else.

I have a friend who was asked to accept a position in her church. She was very talented in that area and thought she might enjoy doing it. So she prayed about it. The Lord said, " No."

"If you accept this job, you will be taking someone else's place and you won't be where I want you to be." We can't second guess God or assume what he wants for us. It's better to ask him first.

As we read the Scriptures, we see that God often surprised his people by what he did.

Who could have been more surprised than Gideon when the angel of the Lord appeared to him?

Whenever the Israelites planted their crops, the Midianites, Amalekites and other eastern people invaded the country. They camped on the land and ruined the crops all the way to Gaza and did not spare a living thing for Israel, neither sheep nor cattle nor donkeys. They came up with their livestock and their tents like swarms of locusts. It was impossible to count the men and their camels;

they invaded the land to ravage it. Midian so impoverished the Israelties that they cried out to the Lord for help.[35]

The angel of the Lord came and sat down under the oak in Ophrah that belonged to Joash the Abiezrite, where his son Gideon was threshing wheat in a winepress to keep it from the Midianites.

When the angel of the Lord appeared to Gideon, he said, "The Lord is with you, mighty warrior."[36]

"Who me?"

Where was Gideon when this happened? Threshing wheat in a winepress to keep it from the Midianites. He was trying to stay out of sight.

He questioned why God had abandoned his people to the Midianites. The Lord turned to him and said, "Go in the strength you have and save Israel out of Midian's hand. Am I not sending you?"[37]

When Gideon was told God was going to use him to lead the Israelites against Midian, he thought he had some pretty good excuses for not doing it.

---

[35] Judges 6:3-6
[36] Judges 6:11-12
[37] Judges 6:14

"But Lord, Gideon asked, "how can I save Israel? My clan is the weakest in Manasseh, and I am the least in my family."[38] He probably wondered, "Why would God choose me?" But he did.

The Lord answered, "I will be with you, and you will strike down all the Midianites together."[39]

When Gideon gathered the Israelites together to fight against their enemies, God said, "You've got too many. We'll have to cut down the number. I'm doing it this way so the Israelites won't think it's their power and strength that wins the battle. They will know it is mine."

The Lord said to Gideon, "You have too many men for me to deliver Midian into their hands. In order that Israel may not boast against me that her own strength has saved her, announce now to the people, 'Anyone who trembles with fear may turn back and leave Mount Gilead.'" So twenty – two thousand men left, while ten thousand remained.[40]

Can you imagine what was going on in Gideon's mind? "What is God doing? I went to all the trouble of rounding up these men and now he is sending some of them home even before the battle begins."

---

[38] Judges 6:15
[39] Judges 6:16
[40] Judges 7:2-3

But the Lord said to Gideon, "There are still too many men. Take them down to the water, and I will sift them for you there. If I say, 'This one shall go with you,' he shall go; but if I say, 'This one shall not go with you,' he shall not go."

So Gideon took the men down to the water. There the Lord told him, "Separate those who lap the water with their tongues like a dog from those who kneel down to drink." Three hundred men lapped with their hands to their mouths. All the rest got down on their knees to drink.

The Lord said to Gideon, "With the three hundred men that lapped I will save you and give the Midianites into you hands. Let all the other men go, each to his own place.[41]

Three hundred men. That isn't very many when you're facing thousands. But Gideon believed God and he saw God's mighty power at work.

Or what about Jehoshaphat? When three armies came against him what did he do? He didn't strategize with his advisors. He immediately turned to God. He confessed he didn't know what to do but said, "My eyes are on you, Lord."

After this, the Moabites and Ammonites with some of the Meunites came to make war on Jehoshaphat.

---

[41] Judges 7:4-7

Some men came and told Jehoshaphat, "A vast army is coming against you from Edom, from the other side of the Sea. It is already in Hazazon Tamar" (that is En Gedi).

Alarmed, (who wouldn't be) Jehoshaphat resolved to inquire of the Lord, and he proclaimed a fast for all Judah.[42] What a wise move on his part. He was greatly outnumbered, but not with God on his side.

First the king reminded God who he is. "Power and might are in your hand, and no one can withstand you."[43]

Then he reminded God that they were his people. "O our God, did you not drive out the inhabitants of this land before your people Israel and give it forever to the descendants of Abraham your friend? They have lived in it and have built in it a sanctuary for your Name, saying, 'If calamity comes upon us, whether the sword of judgment, or plague or famine, we will stand in your presence before this temple that bears your Name and will cry out to you in our distress, and you will hear us and save us.'"[44]

He states the problem and the crisis facing him and with these words we see the key to victory: O our God, will you not judge them? *For we have*

---

[42] 2 Chronicles 20:1-3
[43] 2 Chronicles 20:6b
[44] 2 Chronicles 20:7-9

no power to face this vast army that is attacking us. We do not know what to do, but our eyes are upon you."[45]

Jahaziel prophesies: "Listen, King Jehoshaphat and all who live in Judah and Jerusalem! This is what the Lord says to you: 'Do not be afraid or discouraged because of this vast army. *For the battle is not yours, but God's.*

You will not have to fight this battle. Take up your positions; stand firm and see the deliverance the Lord will give you, O Judah and Jerusalem. Do not be afraid; do not be discouraged. Go out to face them tomorrow, and the Lord will be with you.'"[46] And he was!

Who else but God would have the singers go out ahead of the army praising him! He was their only weapon. That required a great deal of faith on their part. And can you imagine the enemy's shock? That must have caught them by surprise.

After consulting the people, Jehoshaphat appointed men to sing to the Lord and to praise him for the splendor of his holiness as they went out at the head of the army…As they began to sing and praise, the Lord set ambushes against the men of Ammon and Moab and Mount Seir who were invading Judah, and they were defeated.[47]

---

[45] 2 Chronicles 20:12 (Italics mine)
[46] 2 Chronicles 20:15,17 (Italics mine)
[47] 2 chronicles 20:21a, 22

How did God do it? The men of Ammon and Moab turned against Mount Seir and annihilated them. Then they destroyed each other.

God said the fighting men of Israel wouldn't have to use their weapons against the enemy and they didn't. God caused the three armies to turn against one another. All the Israelites had to do was gather up the loot. There was so much plunder, it took three days to do so.

Have you ever been surprised by how God took you through a crisis? I was.

We bought a small lake cottage in the northern part of the state. When we purchased it, we found out there was a drain underneath the house where water from the land above us drained into the lake. We were assured there was nothing to be concerned about. Later, the former owner admitted the drain pipe had rusted out somewhat and one time raccoons had gotten into the house through a small trap door. He insisted the matter had been taken care of, however.

When we bought the cottage, it was on a septic system as were all the others. But the lake association decided all the homes should be converted to sewers and a vacuum system was installed.

One evening, we saw two large raccoons enter an opening at the water's edge and heard them crawling up the drain pipe. We decided it was time to do something about it.

The following spring when we drove up to open the cottage up for the year, we found a small sink hole in our side yard. Concerned about someone falling into it, we filled it in with stones and covered the top of it. Several weeks later while we were there, there was a horrendous storm during the night. When I hurried out early the next morning, I found another sink hole in a different location. This one exposed two pipes in our yard, one of which was much larger than the other. Nothing had been used to seal them together. Instead, someone had flung an unopened bag of dry cement over the place where the two were joined hoping it would do the job. Then he filled in the area around it with dirt. We called the president of the utilities board to come and see what had been done. After looking at it, he gave us a few phone numbers we could call to see if anyone could help us. After calling them, we found no one wanted to get involved.

We were very concerned about the two sink holes and knew we had to do something so we hired a contractor to put in a new drain down the middle of our yard.

John started digging. I prayed that everything would go well and nothing would happen to the vacuum system since he would be scraping very close to it.

He was being very cautious, but all at once he nicked the pipe slightly and it was all downhill from then on. Dirt poured into our vacuum system and systems all up and down the road from us were affected. People were scurrying around to see what had happened.

The manager of the utility company was called and came out. He told us, "You are really in trouble now." They worked diligently to correct the problem but it was going very, very slowly. Finally, he knocked on our door. "We're going to have to go across the road. That will really cost you." Things were going from bad to worse.

I reminded the Lord I had been fervently praying for his help on this whole project. He was the one who told us we had to get it done now. Evidently my prayers weren't doing any good.

Then he said, "You don't understand. Something is wrong on the other side of the road. I had to do it this way so they would check it out. Trust me for this." So I kept on praying.

When they dug up the other side of the road, they found a large rock had fallen against the pipe leading into our yard. One of their own men called us over to see it.

He pointed out, "This is what caused the problem. It wasn't your fault at all." Evidently this had occurred while they were laying the ground work for the vacuum system before we bought the cottage.

The break was corrected, but no one wanted to confront the original contractor. When Hank finally got in touch with his nephew, his reply was, " Oh, we can't be held responsible for that. It's past the two year limitation."

The new drain was put in our yard, the old one removed from under the cottage and the hole leading from it into the lake was plugged up.

We paid John and thought things were settled at last. Shortly afterward, the utility manager knocked on our door and asked if we had paid John yet. When we said yes we had, he said he wanted the check instead.

The following month we received a bill for $1300 for the work the utility company had done. If we disagreed with it, we could appear at their monthly board meeting the next month.

They were quite surprised when Hank walked into the meeting. They didn't know he was coming. I stayed back at the cottage and prayed. Whenever I asked how the meeting was going, the Lord said, "I have already taken care of it."

Since Hank was the only guest, the board decided to let him plead his case first. He explained all that had happened and that we had gotten no support or help from them at all. He told about the dry bag of cement flung over the two different sized pipes, the rock that had broken the vacuum system across the road before we had ever moved in and that our whole summer season from April to September had been spent trying to straighten out the matter.

While the board members were discussing the case, one man spoke up and said, "I recommend we dismiss all the charges. Their whole summer has been ruined." They voted on the motion and it passed. Then the president turned to the utility manager and said, "Now *you* go after the original contractor and get the money."

Hank was stunned. He wondered if he'd heard correctly. He couldn't believe what had happened. They were dismissing all the charges. Then they said, "You can leave now. The case is closed."

When Hank came back from the meeting, he eagerly told me all the details of what happened and we praised the Lord for seeing us through all this. From beginning to end, God had everything under control. He knew what he wanted to accomplish and how it would turn out. His way was certainly different than what we expected. He said he had taken care of everything and he had.

God tells us his ways are different than ours. In what ways have you found this to be true?

We may not understand them. We may disagree with them, but he says they are better than ours. Can you trust him for them?

As we read the Scriptures, we see that God often surprised his people by what he did? Has he ever surprised you? In what ways?

Prayer

Father, I don't understand what's going on now or how it's going to turn out. But one thing I do know: you want your best for me and only you know what that is. I simply trust you for who you are and for your answer to this problem, whatever it is. I pray in the name of Jesus, who showed me how to trust.

CHAPTER
6

WAITING ISN'T EASY

**Wait for the Lord; be strong and take heart
and wait for the Lord.**

Psalm 27:14

WAITING ISN'T EASY

Waiting isn't easy, is it? If we're expecting something good to happen, the days seem like years. If we're anticipating the worst to happen, they seem like mere minutes.

Waiting often becomes a large part of our lives in trying times. But *it is during these periods of waiting, that God shapes us and molds us into what he wants us to be.* He has all the time in the world, yet he will not wait one second too long to bring about what he desires. We are looking for instant results while he is interested in greater benefits for us. He will do it, but there are times he delays things. Our timetable may not be his.

Instead of changing the circumstances, *sometimes he changes us in the circumstances.* We begin to look at them differently and he helps us rise above them.

I've noticed God is as interested in the process as he is the final result. Character is built step by step, decision by decision. Things don't always come easy. That's part of his plan too.

A righteous man may have many troubles, but the Lord delivers him from them all;[48]

---

[48] Psalm 34:19

Think about how long Abraham had to wait before he and Sarah had a son. He was one hundred years old and she was ninety when Isaac was born. It was twenty-five years before God's promise to him was fulfilled. What happened in the meantime?

Yet he did not waver through unbelief regarding the promise of God, but was strengthened in his faith and gave glory to God, being fully persuaded that God had power to do what he had promised. This is why "it was credited to him as righteousness." [49]

I'm sure there were times when Abraham and Sarah wondered if they would ever see the fulfillment of that promise. They even took matters into their own hands to help God out. You know the disastrous results of that.

Some time later after Isaac was born, Abraham faced God's ultimate test. He said to him, "Abraham!" "Here I am," he replied. Then God said, "Take your son, your only son, Isaac, whom you love, and go to the region of Moriah. Sacrifice him there as a burnt offering on one of the mountains I will tell you about." [50]

This was the long awaited son God had promised him and now God was asking him to make the ultimate sacrifice of that same son. Can you imagine the faith it took on Abraham's part to

---

[49] Romans 4:20-22
[50] Genesis 22:1b-2

obey? The Bible doesn't say he questioned God, "I don't understand. How can you ask me to do this?" Nor did he rebel and refuse to do it.

I also think about Isaac and the faith he had in his father. As the two walked along, he asked his father where the sacrificial lamb was. He must have been terribly frightened when Abraham bound him and laid him on the altar on top of the wood and was ready to kill him. He didn't put up a fight when he knew he was to be that sacrifice. Nor did Abraham struggle with his Father as he raised the knife ready to plunge it into his son.

When it really counted, Abraham passed the test. He was willing to sacrifice Isaac, the son of the promise, on the altar to God. He knew that even if he had to kill his son, God could bring him back to life.

By faith Abraham, when God tested him, offered Isaac as a sacrifice. He who had received the promises was about to sacrifice his one and only son, even though God had said to him, "It is through Isaac that your offspring will be reckoned." Abraham reasoned that God could raise the dead, and figuratively speaking, he did receive Isaac back from death.[51]

Consider how long Moses had to wait for God to use him to lead his people out of Egypt. He was forty years old when he ran away to Midean to

---

[51] Hebrews 11:17-19

escape Pharaoh's wrath after killing an Egyptian. He was eighty before God called him to lead his people out of slavery. During those forty years he tended his father-in-law's flocks. God was humbling and preparing him for what lay ahead. God said there was no one else like Moses. (Now Moses was a very humble man, more humble than anyone else on the face of the earth.) [52] God commanded and Moses obeyed.

Since then, no prophet has risen in Israel like Moses, whom the Lord knew face to face, who did all those miraculous signs and wonders the Lord sent him to do in Egypt – to Pharaoh and to all his officials and to his whole land. For no one has ever shown the mighty power or performed the awesome deeds that Moses did in the sight of all Israel. [53]

This is the same Moses who hesitated and made excuses when God called him. "I'm not capable. Send someone else." God didn't. He chose Moses for this very important mission.

God changed Abraham and God changed Moses during those years of waiting. And he wants to change us too.

What happens as I wait on him? *Waiting keeps me focused on him.* As I persist in prayer, that shows him I want the solution as much as he does. I trust him even though I don't know what his answer

---

[52] Numbers 12:3
[53] Deuteronomy 34:10-12

will be. I simply know he wants his best for me and only he knows what that is. I also know he is faithful to all his promises. I just don't know when or how he will bring them about.

Waiting not only matures and builds my faith but my patience as well. Sometimes during these periods, I remind the Lord that Hope deferred makes the heart sick, but a longing fulfilled is a tree of life.[54] When I tell him how long I have been waiting, he replies, "So have I." Then he reminds me how patient he has been with me all these years.

As I wait, I come into an even closer relationship with him. He wants this even more than I do.

He tells me: "I could change everything instantly, but then you wouldn't grow deeper in me."

When I hang in there during the trials, I am also a witness to others. They wonder how I can do that. What do I have that they don't? And I tell them, "It isn't me. It's the Lord. He's the One who holds everything together. I couldn't do it without him"

Sometimes when I'm waiting for God to act, it seems as though I'm treading water and getting nowhere. I'm in limbo. Nothing is happening. We

---

[54] Proverbs 13:12

have a saying in our house, "I feel like I'm walking in molasses," meaning everything I do is so slow and difficult, I'm not moving ahead or getting anything done.

Those are the times he says, "You may not be aware of it, but I am at work right now. Every time you call to me for help, I hear you and answer. You won't see the results for awhile, but I am bringing my solution to your problem. Keep on trusting me for it."

He doesn't abandon or leave us alone during the waiting, but he keeps on encouraging us. It's not a passive waiting – "let's just get through this." It is a positive waiting and we come out stronger having been through it.

Our whole family is well aware of this lesson on waiting. The Lord makes certain we don't miss it. Waiting it out through trying times is not easy. All three of our sons can attest to this as well as my husband and I.

Recently I talked with our son, Bill, about all he and his family have been through. The company he was working for decided to move its operation out of state. Some employees were let go and others given the choice to move with the company.

When he and his wife went to check out the new location, they found housing was higher and the schools were not as good. After much prayer, they felt God was telling them to stay where they are. He would find another job for Bill here.

After making the decision not to move, Bill thought it might be nice to have a few weeks off before job hunting. Little did he know what lay ahead. Those weeks would turn into years.

He plunged into the job hunting process, wrote resumes and tracked down any lead he could find. Nothing. The longer he went without a job, the harder things got. His self worth plummeted. So often our self esteem is linked to what we do. Without a job, who are we? Bill has always been a very hard worker and a good provider for his family. Now there was no job. How was he going to provide for them?

He told me when he was discouraged, he would go into his office at home, shut the door and fall on his face, crying out to the Lord, "You promised me a job. I have to take care of my family. Please, Lord, open the door to the job you have for me. What would you have me do?"

"Trust me and wait on me."

During this time, Bill said his self worth was in the pits. One of the hardest times was picking the boys up at school. People who hadn't seen him for a while asked how things were going and he had to tell them he wasn't working. He dreaded meeting people and having to explain what was going on or rather the lack of it.

He and his family changed churches. Their first church was made up mostly of older people and his children were the only young people there. The change was a good one and this congregation welcomed them warmly. But they had never known Bill when he had a job and wondered why he wasn't employed. He thought some people might consider him lazy since he wasn't working. It was hard on his wife Paula and their three sons. People can unknowingly be cruel by what they say. Sometimes they just don't know what to say.

Hank and I reached out to help and encourage them in any way we could.

A friend called and asked if Bill would be interested in a proposition he was considering. He wanted to buy out his father-in-law's business and put Bill in as manager to run it.

Bill said yes and they began negotiations. Things seemed to be moving steadily ahead. One day Bill met with the son-in-law and his accountant and thought they were deciding the amount to offer for the business. Instead, right in the middle of the meeting, the accountant abruptly said to his client, "I recommend you do *not* buy the business." The friend thought a while, then agreed. All those months spent working on this business proposition went down the tube. Bill was left with nothing except another disappointment. His hopes were dashed again.

When I talked with him later that day he said, "Mom, when I walked out of that meeting, I knew I had to begin praising the Lord or my emotions would have gotten the better of me."

"Lord you know everything that goes on. I don't know why this is happening, but you do. I praise you that you are in charge and you want your best for me. I trust you for the job you have for me. Whatever it is and wherever it is, please bring it to me. I trust you with my life."

That's something else the Lord has been teaching our family: to praise him *in* those times when things are not going right. Praise gets our eyes off us and the problem and on him, the Solver of the problem. It's easy to praise him when everything is going right. It's much more difficult to do so when they aren't.

A position selling alarms for homes opened up and Bill jumped at that. It was difficult making cold calls but he kept at it. However, that job soon dried up since they moved the office out of town. A similar job with another alarm company in town became available and Bill took that, but the future didn't look very promising. The other employees were younger men who quit as soon as they made a little money. They were not in it for the long term.

Finally, after several years, the Lord brought Bill to the company where he wanted him to work. He still isn't in the position God promised him, but he knows it will come. God is faithful to all his promises. His timing is often different than ours.

During this time of waiting, Bill and Paula's faith has deepened and they have no doubts that he is their provider.

God has opened many doors for Bill to give his testimony. It always includes his waiting on the Lord. There have been many times in his life when he has had to wait for God's promises to be fulfilled. Those examples make quite an impact on others, especially young men, because they see Bill's faith lived out in his life.

As parents, we don't like to see our children go through turmoil in their lives. We wish it didn't have to be that way. But it is during those times, we see how God is drawing them closer to him and transforming them into what he wants them to be.

I often find myself in another holding pattern wondering when the waiting will be over so I can go on with the next phase of my life. I don't know when that will be, I simply know it will. And in the meantime, the Lord is at work in me making whatever changes need to be made. He uses this time of waiting to mold me. I still have a long way to go. He is the One who enables me to do so.

<u>Points to Ponder</u>

Waiting isn't easy, but it can be a large part of our lives in trying times.

What is God doing during these periods of waiting? How is he changing us?

Why does he delay the results sometimes? How is that to our benefit?

What happens as we wait on him? How can we emerge stronger in our faith?

<u>Prayer</u>

Sometimes it seems like I've been waiting so long, Father. It's not a question of your doing what you promised. It's not a matter of 'if', but when. I know you timing is different than mine. I'd like to see what you desire now, but you have a good reason for delaying it. I know you won't wait a second too long before bringing it about. And so I wait. My faith is in you, the faithful one. I come to you in Jesus, who showed me what faith is all about.

CHAPTER
7

ATTITUDE MATTERS

You were taught,with regard to your former way of life, to put off your old self, which is being corrupted by its deceitful desires; to be made new in the attitude of your minds; and to put on the new self, created to be like God in true righteousness and holiness.

Ephesians 4:22-24

ATTITUDE MATTERS

In his Word, God clearly shows us that attitude matters.

Through the years, God has humbled our family in order to use us. The trials we've endured have brought us to the point where we depend on him alone and that's exactly where he wants us. We know then and only then can he accomplish his purpose for our lives. He doesn't want us to worry or doubt him. He will provide all we need and more. We are simply to trust him and all that he is.

What a difference there is between trusting him or choosing to depend on ourselves instead.

Two people lose their spouses. One is bitter and never gets beyond it. He lives in the past. The other works through the hurt and grief and moves ahead to the future God has for him.

One person loses his job and remains angry toward the company that let him go. This anger fills his life and seeps into his other relationships as well. Another turns to the Lord when he is terminated, trusts in him and waits for the job God has for him. He sends out resumes, interviews wherever he can, but he knows that ultimately the Lord is the one who will bring him his job.

One continues to relive the past with all of its grievances and complaints. The other lets go of that, lives for today and looks to the future.

One has hope. The other has none. The Lord is that hope.

What does attitude have to do with a crisis? It's at the very heart of it. Attitude has a great deal to do with how you face the crisis and come through it.

Wrong attitudes can help to bring about a crisis. The student who flippantly ignores his home work assignments or consistently misses classes will find himself in a failing position that he brought upon himself. The laborer who does shoddy work and thinks no one will ever know is eventually found out.

Those who consider themselves above the law often find themselves confronted by the law. We've seen and heard a great deal about the lack of ethics in big business.

Attitude comes before action; decision precedes doing.

For as he thinketh in his heart, so *is* he.[55] We are what we think. Sooner or later what's inside is revealed. It exposes what we are really like.

---

[55] Proverbs 23:7 King James

That 's why God tells us: Above all else, guard your heart, for it is the wellspring of life.[56]

What should our attitude be? He not only tells us, but he also gives us the perfect role model to follow…his Son.

Your attitude should be the same as that of Christ Jesus: Who, being in very nature God, did not consider equality with God something to be grasped, but made himself nothing, taking the very nature of a servant, being made in human likeness. And being found in appearance as a man, he humbled himself and became obedience to death – even death on a cross![57]

Why would God come down to live with those he created knowing they will reject and abuse him? Why would he put himself through all that when he already knows how it will turn out?

Jesus is God the Son. They should have been serving him. Yet Jesus had a servant's heart. He told his disciples on the night he was betrayed that he came to serve, not to be served and they were to do the same. They were to follow his example…humility comes before honor.[58]

There's another command Jesus gave to his disciples. He told them to forgive. *He did.* What an

---

[56] Proverbs 4:23
[57] Philippians 2:5-8
[58] Proverbs 15:33b

example he set for us. As he hung on the cross, he forgave those who put him there. "Father, forgive them for they don't know what they're doing". How could Jesus do that? How could he forgive them after all they had done to him?

The Abused forgave those who abused him. The One who was rejected forgave those who rejected him.

Forgiveness is vitally important. Our salvation is based on forgiveness. Jesus died on a cross so we could be forgiven and reconciled to the Father. That's why he came.

We are to forgive as he forgave us. Jesus spoke some very strong words concerning forgiveness.

He said if we don't forgive others, our heavenly Father won't forgive us. If we don't, he won't.

We may have been deeply hurt by someone and find it's impossible to forgive. Only with the Lord's help can we do so.

We may think the other person doesn't deserve to be forgiven. Then we remember, neither do we but God forgave us.

What is our attitude to be? You were taught, with regard to your former way of life, to put off your old self, which is being corrupted by its deceitful desires; to be made new in the attitude of your minds; and to put on the new self, created to be like God in true righteousness and holiness.[59]

Get rid of all bitterness, rage and anger, brawling and slander, along with every form of malice. Be kind and compassionate to one another, forgiving each other, just as in Christ God forgave you.[60]

Do not conform any longer to the pattern of this world, but be transformed by the renewing of your mind. Then you will be able to test and approve what God's will is – his good, pleasing and perfect will.[61] Don't be like the world and look to its values. Be like God and look to his instead.

Therefore, since Christ suffered in his body, arm yourselves also with the same attitude, because he who has suffered in his body is done with sin. As a result, he does not live the rest of his earthly life for evil human desires, but rather for the will of God.[62]

It is very important to be in God's Word everyday. It's vital for a Christ-centered life.

---

[59] Ephesians 4:22-24
[60] Ephesians 4:31-32
[61] Romans 12:2
[62] I Peter 4:1-2

For the word of God is living and active. Sharper than any double-edged sword, it penetrates even to dividing soul and spirit, joints and marrow; it judges the thoughts and attitudes of the heart. Nothing in all creation is hidden from God's sight. Everything is uncovered and laid bare before the eyes of him to whom we must give account.[63]

God knows everything that goes on in our lives. Our motives and actions are exposed and we will be judged on them. That's scary to think about, isn't it? I look forward to meeting Jesus face to face someday. I do not look forward to giving an account of my life and reviewing it from beginning to end. I'm sure there will be many things I'd like to change.

Paul writes to the Colossians and to us as well: Since, then, you have been raised with Christ, set your hearts on things above, where Christ is seated at the right hand of God. Set your minds on things above, not on earthly things. For you died, and your life is now hidden with Christ in God. When Christ, who is your life, appears, then you also will appear with him in glory.[64]

Then he tells them what to get rid of in their lives: Put to death, therefore, whatever belongs to your earthly nature: sexual immorality, impurity, lust, evil desires and greed, which is idolatry…But now you must rid yourselves of all such things as

---

[63] Hebrews 4:12-13
[64] Colossians 3:1-4

these: anger, rage, malice, slander, and filthy language from your lips. Do not lie to each other, since you have taken off your old self with its practices and have put on the new self which is being renewed in knowledge in the image of its Creator.

When we are in Christ, we are supposed to be different than we were before. Therefore, as God's chosen people, holy and dearly loved, clothe yourselves with compassion, kindness, humility, gentleness and patience. Bear with each other and forgive whatever grievances you may have against one another. Forgive as the Lord forgave you. And over all these virtues put on love, which binds them all together in perfect unity.[65]

A change is to take place in our lives, but we aren't the ones who do it. Christ in us, changes us. We cannot change ourselves to live the way he calls us to live. He does it.

My husband and I have been leading Christian seminars for eleven years. One Sunday we traveled to the northern part of the state to conduct a seminar that afternoon.

As we walked into the sanctuary with the minister just before the first morning service was to begin, I noticed two large overstuffed chairs on the platform and a stool nearby. I wondered why they were there. I soon found out.

---

[65] Colossians 3:5,8-10,12-14

I had assumed we would be introduced briefly at both the contemporary and traditional services and the people would be reminded about our seminar that afternoon.

What I had not anticipated was the minister turning to me and saying "By the way, you two are the sermon today. I will be interviewing you in a few minutes."

What a shock that was. We learned this five minutes before the service began. There wasn't time to panic or even worry about what to say. I breathed a silent prayer, "Lord, help us," and released the entire matter into his hands.

Not only were we interviewed in the first service, but the second as well. Individuals from the congregation asked questions and it seemed to go very well. Afterward people came up to talk with us and said how much they had learned from it. *I have absolutely no idea what we said.* The Lord took over completely. It wasn't us, it was him.

Those are the moments when you realize, "Lord there is no way I can do it without you." We don't have to. He is always there. When we call, he answers. I actually enjoyed the interview as we were doing it. I didn't have to be concerned about what to say. I knew the Lord was in charge.

When crises come along, how do we respond to them, struggle through them and what can we learn from them?

I like this Scripture from Psalms: I have set the Lord always before me. Because he is at my right hand, I will never be shaken.[66]

When things happen that shake me, he wants me to be unshakeable in him. That's the key – in him. He is unshakeable.

Nothing is too hard for him. It may be for me, but it isn't for him. Nothing throws him. He is unflappable. He wants me to be unflappable too. I will be as I am in him.

Whatever circumstances I find myself in, he can handle. So I release my concerns to him *every day*. I don't try to carry them alone; I give them to him instead.

The Bible says: … we have the mind of Christ.[67] Our mind is filled with him and we look at things the way he does, from his perspective.

But often our minds are filled with worldly things, those that are decidedly different from the things of Jesus.

---

[66] Psalm 16:8
[67] I Corinthians 2:16b

The mind is a favorite target of Satan. He delights in tempting us, accusing us and making life miserable for us in any way he can. His goal is to separate us from God. Jesus said the devil came to kill and steal and destroy, but that he came to give us life and that abundantly.

God tests us but he never tempts us to do evil. As we go through trials, he matures us and draws us closer to him.

Satan, however, tries to get us to sin, knowing that sin will separate us from God. That's his whole purpose – to get us away from our Creator.

When tempted, no one should say, "God is tempting me." For God cannot be tempted by evil, nor does he tempt anyone; but each one is tempted when, by his own evil desire, he is dragged away and enticed. Then, after desire has conceived, it gives birth to sin; and sin, when it is full-grown, gives birth to death.[68]

Satan enjoys polluting our minds. He does so by various means: putting his thoughts in us, getting us to watch movies and TV we have no business seeing, or reading books and magazines that should have no place in our lives as Christians. Filling our minds with his garbage, dulls our sensitivity to the things of Christ.

---

[68] James 1:13-15

Temptation is not sin. It becomes sins as we think about it and roll it around in our minds and it takes hold of us. Jesus was tempted by the devil when he was here on earth, but he didn't sin. He knows how to help us when we're tempted. We don't have to give in to it either. With his help we won't.

Because he himself suffered when he was tempted, he is able to help those who are being tempted.[69]

No temptation has seized you except what is common to man. And God is faithful; he will not let you be tempted beyond what you can bear. But when you are tempted, he will also provide a way out so that you can stand up under it.[70]

I am amazed at the insidious invasion and deluge of spam and junk mail we are inundated with every day from people we don't even know. Yesterday I had ten spam messges on the internet and today it was up to twenty. As fast as I delete them, there are more. Even our regular mail seems to be ninety percent junk and the paper trail gets longer and longer. My neighbor has a good solution to the problem. After a trip to her mailbox, she stops by the trash can in her garage and sorts out her mail.

---

[69] Hebrews 2:18
[70] I Corinthians 10: 13

Half of it doesn't even make it into the house. She gets rid of it before it does.

Instead of listening to the world or Satan, focus on Jesus.

Finally, brothers, whatever is true, whatever is noble, whatever is right, whatever is pure, whatever is lovely, whatever is admirable – if anything is excellent or praiseworthy – think about such things.[71]

If Jesus were looking over your shoulder right now, would you be watching the video or reading the book you are? When you're filled up with the world, there's no room for him. Right attitudes come from looking at things the way Jesus does. That results in living the life he calls you to live.

---

[71] Philippians 4:8

<u>Points to Ponder</u>

Attitude matters. Why is it so important?

What does it have to do with a crisis?

Attitude comes before action; decision precedes doing. Why does God tell us to guard our hearts above all else?

How can wrong attitudes wreck our lives?

How can the right ones keep us on track?

Where do we look to find out how to live?

<u>Prayer</u>

Father, thank you for your Word. Thank you for instructing and teaching me the way to go, counseling and watching over me. You've given me the guidelines to use, but I need your help to do so. There is so much pollution in the world today. Enable me to keep my mind free of it. Give me the right heart attitude each day as I focus on you instead. Thank you for Jesus, the Living Word. It's in his name that I pray.

CHAPTER 8

WHAT DIFFERENCE DOES HE MAKE?

"Peace I leave with you; my peace I give you. I do not give to you as the world gives. Do not let your hearts be troubled and do not be afraid."

John 14:27

WHAT DIFFERENCE DOES HE MAKE?

What difference does Jesus make in a crisis? Does it really matter if I turn to him when I'm in dire circumstances? Why not tough it out on my own? If I find out I can't make it, then I can always call on him.

That's the attitude of many. We've been taught to be self-reliant, to depend upon ourselves. The world admires the self sufficient man who doesn't think he needs anyone's help.

However, the Bible's perspective is a little different. He who trusts in himself is a fool.[72]

God shakes his head and wonders, "When things are already difficult, why would you choose to make them even harder? When help is available, why do you turn it down?"

"Trust in me with all your heart and don't lean on your own understanding. In all your ways acknowledge me and I will make your paths straight."[73]

Turning to the Lord should be a first response, not a last resort.

---

[72] Proverbs 28:26a
[73] Proverbs 3:5-6 Paraphrase

King David certainly had his share of trials. He didn't live an easy life. As you peruse the Scriptures, you can readily see he faced one trial after another. He often poured out his heart to the Lord.

Find rest, O my soul, in God alone; my hope comes from him. He alone is my rock and my salvation; he is my fortress, I will not be shaken.[74]

My soul clings to you; your right hand upholds me.[75]

The more we can trust God, the more we will trust him. David is a prime example.

The Philistines gathered their forces to fight against the Israelites. They had a champion named Goliath who was over nine feet tall. He towered above everyone else.

For forty days he came out morning and evening to taunt the Israelites. He challenged them to send a man to fight him. No one was about to take the dare.

"If he is able to fight and kill me, we will become your subjects; but if I overcome him and kill him, you will become our subjects and serve

---

[74] Psalm 62:5-6
[75] Psalm 63:8

us."[76] Saul and all his men were terrified and didn't know what to do. Three of David's brothers had followed Saul to war.

Meanwhile, David's father, Jesse, desiring to find out how his sons were doing, sent David to check up on them. He wanted to make certain they were all right.

When David heard Goliath's boasting and defiance against God's army, he volunteered to fight the giant. He said to Saul: "Let no one lose heart on account of this Philistine; your servant will go and fight him."[77]

Saul didn't take him seriously. He pointed out to David that he was only a boy and this giant had been a fighter since his youth. How did he think he could defeat Goliath? The other men were terrified. How did David come by this boldness?

Then David told Saul where his strength came from. The Lord was a vital part of his life.

"Your servant has been keeping his father's sheep. When a lion or a bear came and carried off a sheep from the flock, I went after it, struck it and rescued the sheep from its mouth. When it turned on me, I seized it by its hair, struck it and killed it. Your servant has killed both the lion and the bear; this uncircumcised Philistine will be like one of

---

[76] I Samuel 17:9
[77] I Samuel 17:32

them, because he has defied the armies of the living God. *The Lord who delivered me from the paw of the lion and the paw of the bear will deliver me from the hand of this Philistine.*"

Saul said to David, "Go, and the Lord be with you."[78]

Then he tried to dress David in his tunic, coat of armor and bronze helmet and he gave him his sword, but David said 'no' because he wasn't used to them. They were too cumbersome. Instead he approached the giant with only his staff, five smooth stones and his sling in his hand.

Goliath was insulted when he saw the young boy standing there and said he would quickly make mincemeat of David. This is too easy. "Come here," he said, "and I'll give your flesh to the birds of the air and the beasts of the field!"

David said to the Philistine, "You come against me with sword and spear and javelin, but I come against you in the name of the Lord Almighty, the God of the armies of Israel, whom you have defied. This day the Lord will hand you over to me, and I'll strike you down and cut off your head." (And he did.)

Today I will give the carcasses of the Philistine army to the birds of the air and the beasts of the earth, and the whole world will know that

---

[78] I Samuel 17:34-37 (Italics mine)

there is a God in Israel. All those gathered here will know that it is not by sword or spear that the Lord saves; *for the battle is the Lord's* and he will give all of you into our hands." [79]

David was fired up. As Goliath moved closer to attack him, David ran toward him, took out a stone and slung it, hitting the giant in the head. So David triumphed over the Philistine with a sling and a stone; without a sword in his hand he struck down the Philistine and killed him.

David ran and stood over him. He took hold of the Philistine's sword and drew it from the scabbard. After he killed him, he cut off his head with the sword. [80]

What was the key to victory against such overwhelming odds? David knew his strength was in the Lord. The battle was his.

What about you today? What difference does Jesus make in the crises in your life? What happens when you look to him?

First of all, you are not alone. Regardless of the circumstances, he will see you through them as you turn to him. Two are better than one, especially when one of them is God. God the Son is at the Father's right hand interceding for you. He is cheering you on, pulling for you.

---

[79] I Samuel 17:44-47 (Italics mine)
[80] I Samuel 17:50-51

It's comforting to have someone looking after you and taking care of your needs. And somehow when Jesus is in the picture, those enormous problems that you are facing don't seem so big any more. He has a way of cutting them down to size.

Jesus also gives you his peace right in the middle of the crisis. He says, "I am the eye at the center of the storm. No matter what's going on around you, it is calm where I am. My peace is different from the world's. The world's peace is fragile and can be easily shattered. My peace doesn't depend on what's happening to you or going on all around you. It depends on me. And my peace lasts."

"Peace I leave with you; my peace I give you. I do not give to you as the world gives. Do not let your hearts be troubled and do not be afraid."[81]

When your faith is in him, fear fades.

He is the one who gives you this peace. You can't work it up yourself. As you look to him and trust him, you will have his peace.

His peace is not the absence of problems, but rather him in the midst of those problems.

---

[81] John 14:27

He enables you to rise above and see beyond the circumstances to the victory that lies ahead. He is bigger than any problem. You are not overcome by the situation, you are an overcomer.

Jesus never changes. You can count on him. He is your help and your hope.

Jesus Christ is the same yesterday and today and forever.[82]

There is a sense of awe as you see God working in your life and helping you through the trying times. With all that he has to do, he still makes times for you. Nothing is too small for him to be concerned with. Nothing is too big for him to handle. If it concerns you, it concerns him.

And when you come out on the other side of the ordeal, there is *gratitude and joy*, a joy that only he can give you. So many times I've said, "Lord, you did it. You really did it."

When I said, "My foot is slipping," your love, O Lord, supported me. When anxiety was great within me, your consolation brought joy to my soul.[83]

I knew when I started writing this book about crises, I would undoubtedly have many strewn across my path. And I was right. Some days

---

[82] Hebrews 13:8
[83] Psalm 94:18-19

it's been one thing after the other with new deadlines to meet and wondering how to balance everything else that has to be done. But when I take my focus off the circumstances and get it back on the Lord, I can see he has already begun to work out the situation that confronts me. I praise him for that.

There have been many times when I've said, "Lord, I think I'm in over my head."

And he replies, "But not over mine."

Do you realize how every much he loves you and wants you to succeed? Do you really know how much he cares about you? It pleases him when you come to him with your problems instead of worrying about them or trying to fix them yourself. You may not have the answer, but he does.

I've found when I trust in him, not only is my outlook changed but so are my actions. I'm a different person.

My husband and I have our business in our home so we never really get away from it. There are times when we struggle with a problem and can't seem to come up with an answer. The solution eludes us. We've learned to walk away from it for a little while and take a break with the Lord. We put the dilemma in his hands and ask for his wisdom. Then we begin to praise him that he is already at work to will and to do his good pleasure in this matter.

So often when we've stopped thinking about it, the answer comes. We had been trying so hard, we weren't open to God's solution.

Do not be anxious about anything, but in everything, by prayer and petition, with thanksgiving, present your requests to God. And the peace of God, which transcends all understanding, will guard your hearts and your minds in Christ Jesus.[84]

Concerning his fight with Goliath, David said the battle was the Lord's. Let your crisis be his too. What a difference it makes when it is.

Our son, Bob, lives in the Orlando, Florida area. One Thursday night, he parked his car in his apartment complex and locked it up. The next morning he came out to get in it but it was gone. He knew where he'd parked it but it was nowhere to be found. After looking around the parking area, he realized it had been stolen and called the police.

When the policeman came out to take down all the pertinent information, he mentioned several cars in the general vicinity had been stolen that night. Then he said an alarming thing: "If you car isn't found within the first forty-eight hours, your chances of getting it back are nil. It's either out of the country or chopped up for parts."

---

[84] Philippians 4:6-7

Bob called home and told us what had happened. I prayed with him.

"Father, Bob really needs that car and you know exactly where it is. Please watch over it and keep it safe and bring it back to him as quickly as possible in good drivable condition. Thank you for hearing our prayer and doing so. We come to you in Jesus' name.

I kept thinking his car was close by and so did Bob.

Forty-eight hours came and went and no car, but we kept right on praying. The following Wednesday, Bob got a call from the owner of a gas station three blocks away.

He introduced himself and then asked Bob, "What do you want me to do with your car?"

"What do you mean? I want it back. It's been stolen."

"I didn't know that. It's been sitting here at the station for several days, maybe since last Friday. I kept wondering why no one picked it up so I went to check it out. It's over near a fence so you wouldn't see it if you walked by."

"The lock was broken so I could get into it. I checked the glove compartment, found your name and called you."

Bob thanked him, called the police and walked over to the station. The car was in pretty good condition. The lock was broken and the steering wheel mechanism was damaged where they hot wired it, but it was drivable. In fact, the station owner showed Bob how to hot wire it so he could get over to the garage for repairs. The culprits were never apprehended.

It makes a tremendous difference when you turn to the Lord. He hasn't changed. He is still involved in lives today.

What difference does Jesus make in a crisis? Does it really matter if you turn to him?

What happens when you do?

Turning to the Lord should be a first response, not a last resort. Why do we wait so long?

The more we can trust him, the more we will trust him. Why is that?

Can you recall when he has helped you through a difficult time? Weren't you glad he was there?

Prayer

So many times I've called on you, Lord, and you've always been there. You truly are a very present help in trouble. You always were and always will be, but you are also God of the here and now. I know I'm not alone. And you give me your peace right in the middle of the crisis. When my faith is in you, fear fades away. I come to you in the name of your Son, Jesus, who makes all the difference in the world.

CHAPTER
9

AFTER THE CRISIS, THEN WHAT?

Praise be to the God and Father of our Lord
Jesus Christ, the Father of compassion and the
God of all comfort, who comforts us in all our
troubles, so that we can comfort those in any
trouble with the comfort we ourselves have
received from God.

2 Corinthians 1:3-4

AFTER THE CRISIS, THEN WHAT?

If Jesus makes such a difference in the tough times, why don't we make him an integral part of our lives everyday?

Remember what God said to the Israelites? When the Lord your God brings you into the land he swore to your fathers, to Abraham, Isaac and Jacob, to give you—a land with large, flourishing cities you did not build, houses filled with all kinds of good things you did not provide, wells you did not dig, and vineyards and olive groves you did not plant—then when you eat and are satisfied, be careful that you do not forget the Lord, who brought you out of Egypt, out of the land of slavery.[85]

He was saying, "You call on me when you're in trouble and I help you. Don't forget me when everything is going right."

God could say the same thing to us today. When is the hardest time to turn to him? When things are going well. We don't think we need him then. But we never outgrow our need for him and his Son.

Sam's marriage was falling apart. He and Sally were newlyweds, but after two months she was bored with it all.

---

[85] Deuteronomy 6:10-12

Sally loved the anticipation, the thrill and excitement of bridal showers. She thrived on being the focus of all that attention. The wedding and reception were beautiful and expensive.

But the day to day responsibilities and reality of married life did not appeal to her. That wasn't what she had in mind. She was ill prepared for what marriage is all about. Sally wanted a continual life of fun and excitement and she took her wedding vows lightly.

Sam, on the other hand, took his very seriously. He loved Sally and wanted to make their marriage work. He switched jobs in order to make more money to please her. They tried counseling but to no avail. It takes two who are willing to work at it. Nothing seemed to satisfy her.

As if his failing marriage weren't enough, there was also the possibility that Sam might lose his job. The company he worked for was cutting back.

One morning Sam called and asked us to pray for him. His boss had scheduled a meeting with him later that day. He thought his job might be terminated.

A few months before this, I had given him cards with pertinent Scripture verses written on them. I cut them into the size of credit cards so they would fit into his wallet and he could carry them

with him all the time. If he got discouraged, he was
to pull out a verse that reminded him God loved him
and was there for him wherever he was, even at
work. He told us he used those cards quite often.

Sam called that night to relate what had
happened. He said, "As I was waiting for that
meeting, I decided to read those verses again. I
pulled out the card with 'I am the Lord, the God of
all mankind. Is anything too hard for me?'[86] And I
thought, no. Nothing is too hard for you, God. That
got me excited."

"Then I looked at another of my favorites:
Do not be anxious about anything, but in
everything, by prayer and petition, with
thanksgiving, present your requests to God. And the
peace of God which transcends all understanding
will guard your hearts and minds in Christ Jesus."[87]

He said, "After reading those verses, I was
so pumped up. I walked into that meeting filled with
God's peace. He was right there with me. I knew if
I lost my job, God would bring me another one."

Months later when we talked with Sam
about his impending divorce and all that was going
on in his life he said, " I wouldn't want anyone to
go through what I have. It's awful. And yet I
wouldn't have missed it for the world. My faith in
the Lord has grown so strong and I know my Lord

---

[86] Jeremiah 32:27
[87] Philippines 4:6-7

is always with me. I used to think this was the worst year of my life. Now I know it's probably been the best. I'm so glad I learned this now in my twenty's rather than later."

Then he added, "When things return to normal, I don't ever want to lose the closeness with the Lord that I have now."

Tough times are hard to take, but that's when we grow the fastest and the deepest. The lessons the Lord has been teaching us take hold and spill over into our lives each day.

What did Sam learn during those months? First of all, he learned that his Lord was there for him and he was the One who took him through those devastating times. He didn't go through them alone.

His faith grew stronger to a depth he had never known before. It had been tested and tried and remained true. He trusted the Lord for seeing him through all this and he could trust him in the future.

Faith is being sure of what we hope for, certain of what we do not see.[88]

Sam's faith became fact. It isn't, "I think God will always be there for me. I sure hope he is." It is no longer a theory, but "I know he will. Now I

---

[88] Hebrews 11:1

have seen him at work in my life, therefore I can trust him with my future."

He also learned it is possible to have God's peace right in the middle of the chaos. His peace doesn't depend on what's happening to us or going on around us. It depends on him.

Sam's relationship with the Lord became stronger. He doesn't want to lose that closeness he has now. This young man knows how important it is and that the quality of his life depends on where Jesus Christ is in it.

But when the crisis is over, what then? How do you keep that closeness with the Lord that you had through the turmoil and tribulations? How can you keep it from slipping away? As we look back, we are so grateful for what he has done. But time and the busyness of life have a way of dulling our memories. We get caught up with other things and sometimes we forget.

We mean to keep in touch with the Lord when the difficult times are over but we can lose that intimacy with him. Good intentions don't count. They aren't enough. Our relationship with him doesn't stay the same. It doesn't stand still. We are either growing closer to him or else we are moving farther away. Sometimes we don't even realize it until much later. *Something is missing in our lives when he is.*

How do we continue to keep close to the Lord? *By spending time with him each day.* I've found the most crucial part of my day is time spent with him. It sets the tone for the rest of the day. I do so before the urgency of the morning hits me. I also end the day with him, reflecting on and thanking him for all he has done for me. In fact, I include him in every part of my life – the good times as well as those when I need his help.

So then, just as you received Christ Jesus as Lord, continue to live in him, rooted and built up in him, strengthened in the faith as you were taught and overflowing with thankfulness.[89]

Reading his Word is vital. A daily dose makes quite a difference. He reveals himself to us in his Word. Who is better qualified to do so than he? He also shows us what we are like. Some of it we may not like to hear. Man hasn't changed that much through the years. We are still sinners in need of a Savior. He also gives us his guidelines by which to live. When we follow them, things go much better.

It's comforting to know he is always available. We never get a busy signal. He doesn't put us on hold while he takes another call. And there isn't a maze of menus to muddle through. He hears our prayers when we pray. He listens and answers. Consider how much trouble he went to so we can come to him. How disappointed he must be when we don't.

---

[89] Colossians 2:6

We say we are too busy for that. "You should see my day-timer. It's chucked full of all I have to do." Think about it. We make time for those things we *have* to do. And we make time for those things we *want* to do. Why not make time with him a top priority? When we were going through the crisis we did. Why not now when it's over?

Sam is reaching out to several young men who found themselves in similar circumstances to his. He is using his painful experience to help others. How encouraging his faith has been to them. They look at him and think, "You made it through with God's help and so can I. If he was there for you, I believe he will be there for me too." The Lord brought good out of a bad situation.

Praise be to the God and Father of our Lord Jesus Christ, the Father of compassion and the God of all comfort, who comforts us in all our troubles, so that we can comfort those in any trouble with the comfort we ourselves have received from God.[90]

I just finished talking with a woman from our church who is making a big difference in the lives of others.

When Karen's husband died a few years ago, there was no support group for those whose spouses had died. Out of her grief she and another woman started one for both men and women who had recently lost their mates. Through the years it

---

[90] 2 Corinthians 1:3-4

has flourished and continues to grow. People from other churches heard about it and attend.

Those in the group are nourished and fed both physically, and spiritually. The focus is on the Lord, their Helper in times of need.

The bond is also strong among the members. Even though many have moved on with their lives, they still like to get together with the group for picnics and other social occasions. They are like family. Just as the Lord helped Karen through her heartache, he is using her to help them.

What about you? After the crisis is over, what then? What will you do? God doesn't leave. He is still there waiting to take you through the next phase of your life.

After the crisis is over, then what? Where do you go from there?

How has your life changed?

God told the Israelites they called on him when they were in trouble and he helped them. "Don't forget me when everything is going right." He could say the same thing to us today.

How do you keep the closeness you had with the Lord during the turmoil and trials?

How might he have you reach out to others who are going through similar experiences?

Prayer

Father, I am so grateful for you and all your help. I couldn't have made it through this without you. Show me what the next step is in my life. I want to always have that closeness I have with you now. I don't want to lose it. Use me in any way to show others how much you love and care about them. Make me a reflection of your Son. It's in his name I pray.

CHAPTER
10

IT PAYS TO OBEY!

To obey is better than sacrifice,

I Samuel 15:22b

IT PAYS TO OBEY

I remember when I first discovered the strong correlation between love and obedience. I was teaching a Bible class in our home. Each week the Lord would give me the lesson I was to teach. First I had to learn it before I could teach others.

I'd read the same Scriptures before, but somehow this time they penetrated more deeply. They struck a chord with me. The words were the same, but their meaning became much sharper and clearer.

Jesus said, "If you love me, you will obey what I command." [91]

Then he continued: "Whoever has my commands and obeys them, he is the one who loves me. He who loves me will be loved by my Father, and I too will love him and show myself to him."[92]

Who could ask for more than that? Not only do I show my love for Jesus as I obey him, but he will love me and reveal himself to me. And the Father will love me too. That pleases him as I love his Son.

---

[91] John 14:15
[92] John 14:21

"If anyone loves me, he will obey my teaching. My Father will love him, and we will come to him and make our home with him. He who does not love me will not obey my teaching. These words you hear are not my own; they belong to the Father who sent me."[93]

I pondered, "If obeying shows I really love you, Lord, what happens when I don't? Does that mean the love I profess for you is merely lip service and it's not from my heart? I want my love for you lived out in my life."

This is love for God: to obey his commands. And his commands are not burdensome.[94]

I also found out obedience ties in with knowing him. We know that we have come to know him if we obey his commands. The man who says, "I know him," but does not do what he commands is a liar and the truth is not in him.[95]

Those are strong words. We can't fool God. He looks straight into our hearts. If what we say isn't lived out by what we do, it lacks credibility. He knows we don't mean it.

Jesus asked: "Why do you call me, 'Lord, Lord,' and do not do what I say?"

---

[93] John 14:23-24
[94] I John 5:3
[95] I John 2:3-4

"I will show you what he is like who comes to me and hears my words and puts them into practice. He is like a man building a house, who dug down deep and laid the foundation on rock. When a flood came, the torrent struck that house but could not shake it, because it was well built."

"But the one who hears my words and does not put them into practice is like a man who built a house on the ground without a foundation. The moment the torrent struck that house, it collapsed and its destruction was complete."[96] *It pays to obey.*

King Saul found out what happens when you disobey God. He lost his kingship. God had appointed him king of Israel, but he took it away when Saul failed to follow his commands.

Samuel said to Saul, "I am the one the Lord sent to anoint you king over his people Israel; so listen now to the message from the Lord. This is what the Lord Almighty says: 'I will punish the Amalekites for what they did to Israel when they waylaid them as they came up from Egypt. Now go, attack the Amalekites and totally destroy everything that belongs to them. Do not spare them; put to death men and women, children and infants, cattle and sheep, camels and donkeys.'"[97]

Then Saul attacked the Amalekites all the way from Havilah to Shur, to the east of Egypt. He

---

[96] Luke 6:46-49
[97] I Samuel 15:1-3

took Agag king of the Amalekites alive, and all his people he totally destroyed with the sword. But Saul and the army spared Agag and the best of the sheep and cattle, the fat calves and lambs – everything that was good. These they were unwilling to destroy completely, but everything that was despised and weak they totally destroyed.[98]

God was very displeased with Saul and what he had done. Then the word of the Lord came to Samuel: "I am grieved that I have made Saul king, because he has turned away from me and has not carried out my instructions."[99]

Samuel went to confront Saul the next day. When he saw him, Saul said, "The Lord bless you! I have carried out the Lord's instructions."

But Samuel said, "What then is this bleating of sheep in my ears? What is this lowing of cattle that I hear?[100]

In his own mind, Saul thought he had complied with God's commands. And when Samuel asked, "What about the sheep and cattle I hear?" Saul came up with an unacceptable excuse.

Saul answered, "The soldiers brought them from the Amalekites; they spared the best of the

---

[98] I Samuel 15:7-9
[99] I Samuel 15:10-11a
[100] I Samuel 15:13-14

sheep and cattle to sacrifice to the Lord your God, but we totally destroyed the rest.”

“Stop!” Samuel said to Saul. “Let me tell you what the Lord said to me last night.”

The Lord anointed you king over Israel. And he sent you on a mission, saying, ‘Go and completely destroy those wicked people, the Amalekites; make war on them until you have wiped them out. Why did you not obey the Lord? Why did you pounce on the plunder and do evil in the eyes of the Lord?”[101]

Saul still didn’t get it. He continued to claim he did what God called him to do. In his own eyes he had been obedient.

“But I did obey the Lord,” Saul said. “I went on the mission the Lord assigned me. I completely destroyed the Amalekites and brought back Agag their king. The soldiers took sheep and cattle from the plunder, the best of what was devoted to God, in order to sacrifice them to the Lord your God at Gilgal.”[102]

He mistakenly believed that by making a big show of sacrificing to God everything would be smoothed over and God would be satisfied. But he wasn’t.

____

[101] I Samuel 15:15-16,17b-19
[102] I Samuel 15:20-21

Then Samuel let Saul know how very important obedience is to God and what a horrible mistake he made.

But Samuel replied: "Does the Lord delight in burnt offerings and sacrifices as much as in obeying the voice of the Lord? *To obey is better than sacrifice*, and to heed is better than the fat of rams. For rebellion is like the sin of divination, and arrogance like the evil of idolatry. Because you have rejected the word of the Lord, he has rejected you as king."

Then Saul said to Samuel, "I have sinned. I violated the Lord's command and your instructions. I was afraid of the people and so I gave in to them."[103]

That's a lesson for each of us to keep in mind. Obedience is very important to God. What he thinks of us is of far greater worth than what others do. How we look in his eyes is more significant then how we appear to others.

I've also learned *delayed obedience is disobedience.* When God tells us to do something, we need to do it then, not later.

We used to have a silver Toyota Corolla. It was a very good car for us but had quite a few miles on it. My husband suggested that we should get a

---

[103] I Samuel 15:22-24 (Italics mine)

new one. We prayed about it and the answer was affirmative.

But later as I thought about it again, I concluded it still had some good years left and put the idea aside. Meanwhile Hank checked several dealerships to see if they had any good buys. I felt we shouldn't be in a hurry as the car was still running well.

During this time I led a small group in prayer on Wednesday mornings at our church. One Wednesday when we had finished, a friend from the group and I were going out for lunch. She left ahead of me and I was to meet her at the restaurant.

I left the church, but had to stop for a red light. As I turned the corner onto a very crowded thoroughfare and started to shift gears, I discovered I no longer had a clutch. Without a clutch, I couldn't shift or move forward. I tried to maneuver to one side but didn't quite make it. I quickly turned on the hazard lights. I was also concerned about my friend. She would be waiting at the restaurant wondering what had happened to me.

There in the middle of a very busy street, the Lord spoke very clearly to me. *"Now are you ready to get a new car?"*

"Yes," I said with no hesitation. "Lord, forgive me for my reluctance in obeying you. Please just get me out of here."

"I will get you to the restaurant and I will get you home afterward. However, do not run the errands you had planned to. Go straight home after your lunch."

I met my friend and had a nice lunch. The car seemed to be working well and for a moment I considered getting my errands done. Again the Lord said, "Go straight home." So I did.

I called the Toyota garage about bringing the car in the next day. They asked if they needed to pick it up. I said, "No problem, I can get it there."

When Hank got home that night, I told him what had happened. I used his car to get my shopping done. I also told him not to use the Toyota.

I got in the car early the next morning to take it to be repaired. It started right up and I was on my way … *for half a block.* Again I had no clutch. So I walked back home and called the Toyota garage to bring their flatbed truck. I couldn't make it there after all.

The mechanic fixed the master clutch cylinder and *we went out to buy a new car.*

It is serious business when we disobey the Lord. He knows what is best for us. He wanted to give us a new car, but I wasn't willing to take it. I was quite satisfied with the old one.

There have been times in my life when the Lord asked, "Why do I have to push you through the door of opportunity?" I am learning to say yes as he opens the door.

He continues to teach me about two very important truths. Believe and obey. I can't please him without faith nor can I please him without obedience.

The book of Romans refers to the obedience that comes from faith. If I truly believe him, then I will obey him. There is no other way.

Jesus Christ in my life makes all the difference in the world, not only in the crises, but in the good times as well. One of the things I appreciate about him the most – he is always there for me in the crises and out of them.

<u>Points to Ponder</u>

Why is obedience so important to God? Why does it pay to obey?

How does loving him tie in with obeying him?

What is the connection between obeying him and knowing him?

The book of Romans refers to the obedience that comes from faith. We can't please God without faith nor can we please him without obedience. If we truly believe him, we will obey him.

<u>Prayer</u>

Father, thank you for teaching me about the importance of believing you and obeying you. I choose to do so, but I need your help each day to live it out. I also know that delayed obedience is disobedience. Enable me to do what you tell me to do when you tell me to do it. I pray in the name of Jesus, the epitome of obedience, the perfect example.

ABOUT THE AUTHOR

Mary Ann Kiszla is an author as well as a conference and convention speaker who shows what a difference Jesus Christ makes in our lives. She was in charge of the Prayer Ministry in a large church for five years and worked with many who were going through crises.

She and her husband are founders of As One Ministries and lead Christian seminars. She is a graduate of DePauw University.

Her books include IN HIS HANDS, AND THE WINNER IS, THE ANSWER TO STRESS, PRAYER GOD'S PERSPECTIVE AND OURS, YOU ARE PRECIOUS IN HIS SIGHT and WHAT DOES GOD SAY?